MINISTRY OF MUNITIONS.

**Technical Department—Aircraft Production.**

**PFALZ TYPE DXII.**

I.C. 653.

Report on the

PFALZ (Type DXII) SINGLE SEATER

FIGHTER.

OCTOBER, 1918.

J. G. WEIR,
Brigadier-General,
Controller, Technical Department.

The Naval & Military Press Ltd

Published by
**The Naval & Military Press Ltd**
5 Riverside, Brambleside, Bellbrook
Industrial Estate, Uckfield, East Sussex,
TN22 1QQ England

Tel: +44 (0) 1825 749494
Fax: +44 (0) 1825 765701

www.naval-military-press.com
www.military-genealogy.com

*In reprinting in facsimile from the original, any imperfections are inevitably reproduced
and the quality may fall short of modern type and cartographic standards.*

## MINISTRY OF MUNITIONS.

## Technical Department—Aircraft Production.

I.C. 653.

PFALZ TYPE DXII.

# Report on the
# PFALZ (Type DXII) SINGLE SEATER FIGHTER.

## OCTOBER, 1918.

J. G. WEIR,
Brigadier-General,
Controller, Technical Department.

# REPORT ON THE PFALZ (DXII) SINGLE SEATER FIGHTER.

This aeroplane, which is allotted G/H.Q/6, was brought down near Dury, on 15/9/18; by Lt. Cameron (No. 1 Squadron) and Capt. Staton (No. 62 Squadron).

Although in construction it is strongly reminiscent of the Nieuport-like type of Pfalz which was reported on in I.C. 636, the design if this machine is entirely new, and is of considerable interest.

## GENERAL DESIGN.

As will be seen from the General Arrangement drawings at the end of this Report, the DXII Pfalz has a car-type radiator in front of the engine, and wings which have two bays a side. The lower planes are faired off into the body in the characteristic Pfalz way, but the fin, which in the earlier model was built of 3-ply as an integral part of the body, is now a separate fitting.

| | |
|---|---|
| Area of upper wings (without ailerons) | 104.8 sq. ft. |
| Area of lower wings (both) | 117.6 sq. ft. |
| Area of aileron (one only) | 8.4 sq. ft. |
| Area of balance of aileron | .8 sq. ft. |
| Area of elevators (each) | 8.4 sq. ft. |
| Area of balance of elevator (one) | .6 sq. ft. |
| Area of rudder | 8.8 sq. ft. |
| Area of balance of rudder | .4 sq. ft. |
| Area of tail plane (both sides) | 16.0 sq. ft. |
| Area of fin | 4.4 sq. ft. |
| Area of body (horizontal) | 32.8 sq. ft. |
| Area of body (vertical) | 53.6 sq. ft. |
| Engine | 180 H.P. Mercedes. |
| Petrol capacity | 18¾ gallons. |
| Guns | Two Spandau (fixed). |

The portion of body 3-ply which bears an inscription regarding weight and permissible load is missing.

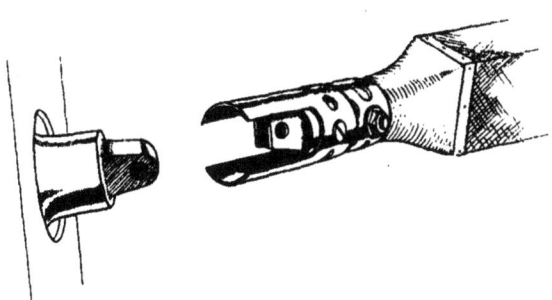

Fig. 1.

## WINGS.

The flat upper plane is built in one piece as before, but the centre section contains neither gravity tank nor radiator, and the tips are no longer heavily raked. The two ailerons of high aspect ratio, are very similar to those of the DVII. Fokker, as are the placing of the radiator and the form of the interplane struts.

The lower planes, which are attached to a kind of centre section that may be said to grow out of the body, are of the same chord as the upper plane, and only slightly shorter in span. The lower planes possess a dihedral angle, in this case of 1½ deg., and the two pairs of interplane struts on each side slope outwards.

The attachments of the lower plane to the body are unchanged. From Fig. 1 it will be seen that the spars are cut down to circular section at their extremities, and a piece of steel tube is bolted over.

Fig. 2.

A lug on the fuselage has a circular-section base round which the open end of the tube on the spar fits, while the lug itself is pinned into the fork on the spar in the usual manner. Both front and rear spars are attached in this way.

Fig. 2 shows the upper aerofoil section compared with that of the R.A.F. 14, which is shown dotted. It will be noticed that the two sections approximate more closely than was previously the case.

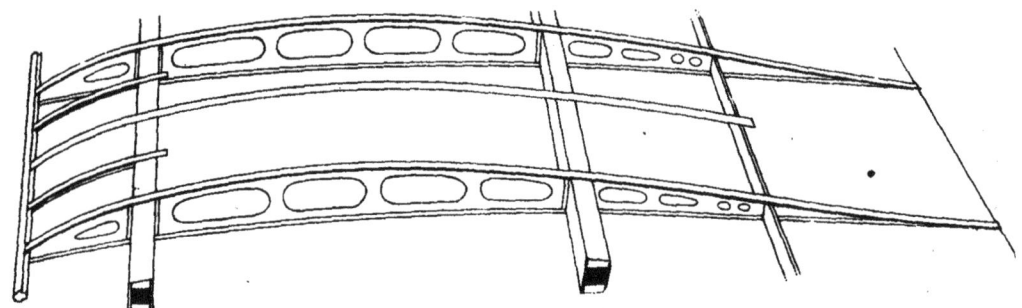

Fig. 3.

The wing construction of upper and lower planes is similar. Each lower wing contains eleven ribs, spaced at equal intervals of approximately $13\frac{1}{2}$ in. The wood leading edge of the plane is not of the usual "C" section, but is more solid, as will be noticed from Fig. 3. The spars retain the former Pfalz design, but the section is of a squarer shape than formerly, and the flanges are not spindled. Dimensioned sketches are given in Fig. 4, and the upper and lower plane spars are exactly similar. At those points where the strut attachments occur, the spars are solidified by the insertion of small blocks of wood, as shown in the lower sketch of Fig. 4. The various components of the spars are very strongly glued together with a casein cement, and fabric is glued round the whole.

The tape lattice work that was found in the old-type Pfalz between the spars, and between the rear spar and trailing edge is no longer present, but a vertical rectangular-section strip of wood lies parallel to the rear spar between that member and the trailing edge, and strips of wood are tacked on to the leading edge, and on to the two spars, and finish just behind this strip. These false ribs are placed midway between the true ribs, and the space between each false and true rib is again bisected by another strip. These pieces simply pass from the leading edge to just behind the front spar, and are built up with a vertical strip so that the whole is of T section. The ribs are of 2 mm. 3-ply, with flanges tacked on in the usual way, and are lightened to the extent shown in Fig. 3, which explains clearly all the features just described. The trailing edge is of wire, and each rib has fabric sewn over it. There are twelve steel compression tubes in the upper plane, and five in each of the lower planes. The bracing varies from steel tie rods of 5 mm. diameter to 12-gauge piano wire.

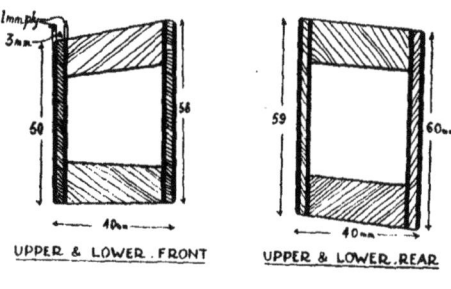

UPPER & LOWER FRONT    UPPER & LOWER REAR

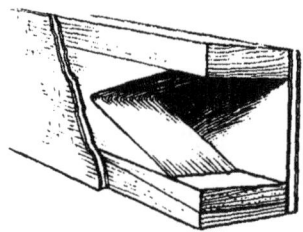

Fig. 4

## AILERONS.

The ailerons, which are fitted only to the uper wings, are very similar to those of the DVII. Fokker. They are balanced, and their high aspect ratio can be judged from the General Arrangement drawings. They are constructed of light welded steel tube, and have the usual welded-up curved aileron lever, which works in a slot cut in the plane. The hinges

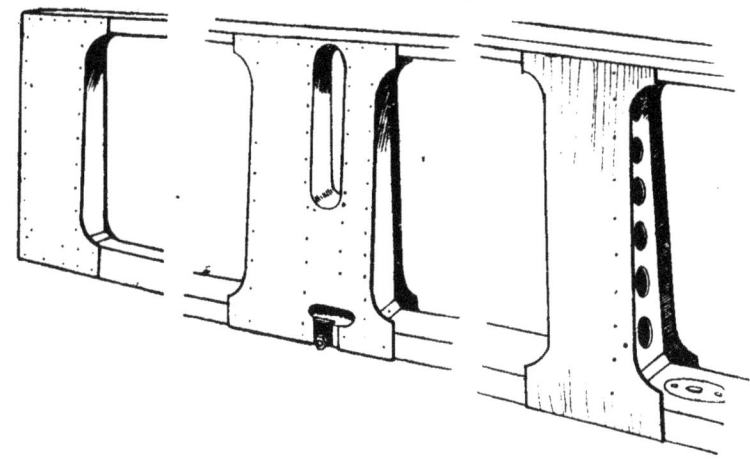

Fig. 5.

by which the ailerons are attached are very simple. A length of $\frac{3}{16}$ in. mild steel rod passes through eyebolts fixed alternately to the wing and aileron, and is secured at one end by a knob, and at the other end by a split pin. Fig. 5 shows how strongly the false spar, to which the aileron is hinged, is coupled to the rear spar.

## STRUTS.

All the interplane struts of the DXII. are of streamline steel tube, and not of wood as before. The centre section struts take the form of two "M's," as is clearly shown by the side view in the scale drawings. A slight adjustment is possible at the three central points, by the means already mentioned in the Report on the Fokker biplane. i.e., there is a nut welded to the point of the strut, and a ball-headed bolt is screwed in. The ball, which is drilled, fits into a pierced round socket, and a small bolt locks the joint.

The interplane struts are of precisely similar design to those of the DVII. Fokker, and are of N-shape when seen from the starboard side of the machine. They slope outwards from bottom to top, but, since the spars are equal distances apart in top and bottom planes, the front and rear limbs are parallel. They are attached to the spars by similar joints to those of the centre section, but in this case the strut carries the cup, and the spar has the ball-headed bolt passing through from top to bottom. Fig. 6 shows the spar fitting, and explains the manner in which the bracing is fixed by a dome held down by the bolt. The diameter and width of the struts, both centre section and interplane, are marked on a diagram, Fig. 7. The gauge of the metal has not been measured.

The wings are braced with the usual flying and landing cables, and besides these it will be noticed from the scale drawings, that a lift wire is fitted between the lower rear spar and fuselage joint at the lower end, and the upper rear spar and centre section strut at the upper end. The lower front spar root is also joined by a cable to a lug fixed a few inches from the front of the engine bearers.

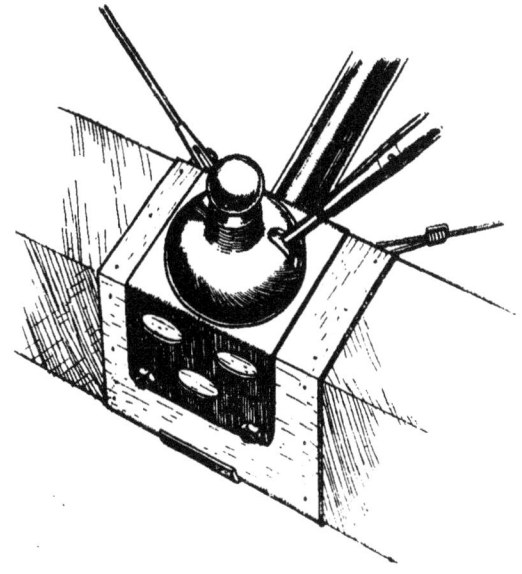

Fig. 6.

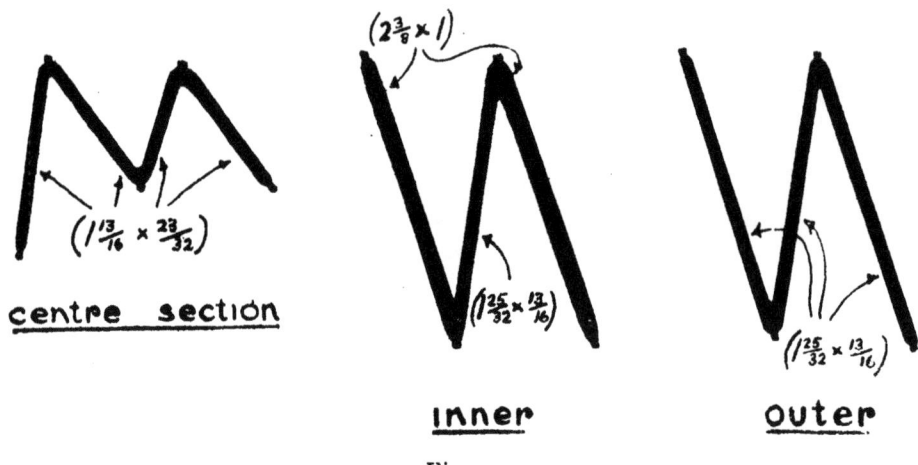

Fig. 7.

## FUSELAGE.

It is interesting to note that, although many drastic alterations between the D III. Pfalz and the new type have been made, the method of construction employed for the fuselage has not been changed.

The body is of oval section, deeper in proportion to its width than before, and has eight lightened longerons, to which are fixed lightened cross bulkheads. Over this framework, two thin 3-ply skins are tacked spirally, as was described in the D III. Pfalz Report. The body is entirely without internal wire bracing. There is a strong bulkhead immediately behind the engine, and forward of this the 3-ply skin drops almost to the level of the engine bearers, as may be seen in the photographs. The sides of the engine are enclosed by aluminium cowls, and the front is covered by the radiator. An aluminium cowl rounds off the lower part of the nose, and joins the 3-ply of the body.

The pilot's seat is missing, but it was supported on a steel tubular framework, which remains, and is illustrated in Fig. 8. It should be noticed from this sketch, that the seat is adjustable both horizontally and vertically, there being three possible positions horizontally, and two vertically. The pilot's backrest is a simple strip of webbing attached to the sides of the fuselage, and the anchorage points for the safety belt are exactly as on the D III. machine. The body tapers consistently towards the rear, and finishes in a vertical knife-edge, about 16 in. deep.

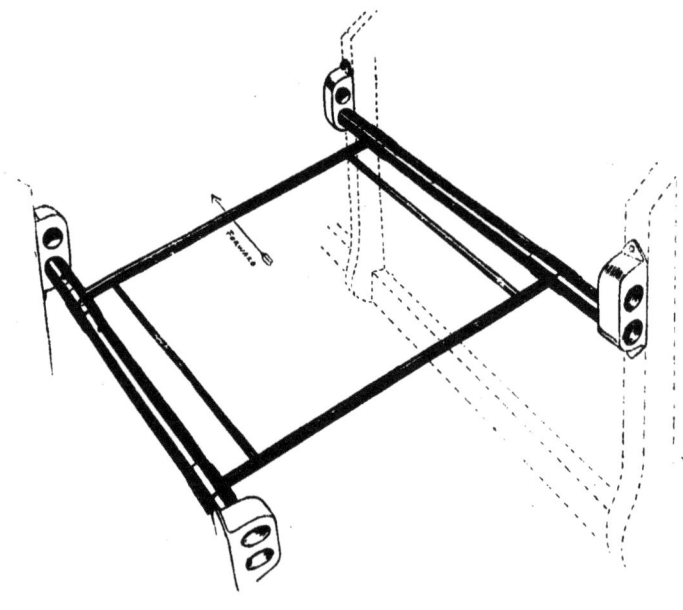

Fig. 8.

## TAIL.

The body and fin are no longer integral, as in the D III., but the fin is simply a self-contained unit of welded-steel tube and fabric, bolted into its place. The fixed horizontal tail plane, however, is integral with the body, although the joint between fuselage and tail plane is an abrupt angle. The tail plane spars pass right through the body, and are connected by ribs lightened roughly by the boring of many circular holes,

Not only is the angle of incidence of the tail plane not adjustable, but the plane is incapable of removal. The camber is symmetrical, and its centre line is not only parallel to, but also in line with the crankshaft.

The balanced and divided elevators (in the D III. the elevator was in one piece) are hinged by a means similar to the aileron hinges, and from the sketch, Fig. 10, which shows the manner of removal of the hinge-rod, it will be noticed that the leading edge of the elevator is a steel tube, flattened to a vertical oval in the unbalanced portion, and to a horizontal oval in the balanced piece. The elevators are constructed throughout of welded steel tube, and the balanced rudder has the same construction.

The tail skid is a sturdy piece of ash with the usual steel shoe, and is balanced about its middle. The upper half is encased in the fuselage, and the shock absorber is of double coil steel spring.

Fig. 9 shows the framework construction at the rear of the fuselage.

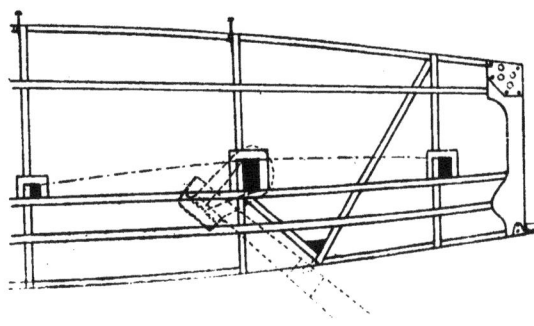

Fig. 9.

## UNDERCARRIAGE.

This component was not salved, and in the scale drawings the D III. undercarriage has been supplied, as the two are conjectured to be substantially similar. From the sockets on the fuselage, it is clear that the limbs of the under carriage vee finished in ball joints.

The following particulars regarding the undercarriage are taken from a French source. It is of the same type as that shown in dotted lines in the scale drawings, but the centre line of the axle is vertically underneath the leading edge of the lower planes, and $31\frac{1}{2}$ in. below this leading edge at the centre section. The track is given as 61 in. in the French drawings.

## ENGINE AND MOUNTING.

The engine, a 180 h.p. Mercedes (reported to be No. 42932, B.N. 827, M.N. 63, guaranteed till 30/1/19), is carried on rectangular-section ash bearers ($3\frac{5}{16}$in. × $1\frac{1}{2}$in.), which are lightened in places to I section. At the front end, the bearers project a few inches beyond the U-shaped front bulkhead. Two other similarly-shaped bulkheads support the bearers in the places shown by dotted lines in the side view of the scale drawings, and at the rear the bearers are mortised into the behind-engine bulkhead, so that the end of the bearers are flush with the rear surface of the bulkhead. The top of the bearers is covered on either side with a 3-ply shelf which extends to the side of the fuselage. In the three-quarter front view photograph may be seen an aluminium scoop (there is also one on the starboard side), which leads air round the crankcase for cooling purposes. The air escapes by holes which are visible just above the leading edge of the lower plane.

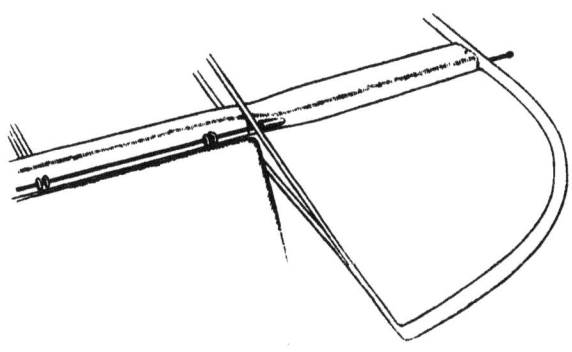

Fig. 10.

## RADIATOR.

The radiator no longer occupies the position it had on the D III. model—i.e., in the centre section—but now closely follows Fokker practice. Fig. 11 shows the shape and construction, and it will be noticed that the whole radiator is situated above the crankshaft. The tank at the head of the radiator is of sheet brass, covered with an aluminium lacquer.

The construction, it will be observed, is very simple. A large number of oval-section tubes of thin brass (9 mm. × 4 mm. cross section), are arranged vertically between the header tank and the radiator bottom, and are supported by two intermediate shelves. The tubes are staggered, and have their cross section inclined at a slight angle to the line of flight, so that the air currents have no straight path, but must impinge upon all the tubes in their course through the radiator. There is a peculiar aluminium "blinker" on the starboard side, permanently fixed edge-wise to the line of flight. Its probable purpose is to prevent the propeller swirl from altogether missing the starboard part of the radiator, by deflecting the current.

The fact that it is fixed on the starboard side, and that the propeller turns in an anti-clockwise direction when seen from the front, gives support to this view.

Two aluminium shutters are fitted behind the radiator, one each side—the tops can be seen in Fig. 11—and are worked positively and independently by means of cables.

The radiator is supported by two sheet-steel brackets, which are fitted to the foremost bulkhead, a few inches above the engine bearers. (See three-quarter front view photograph.)

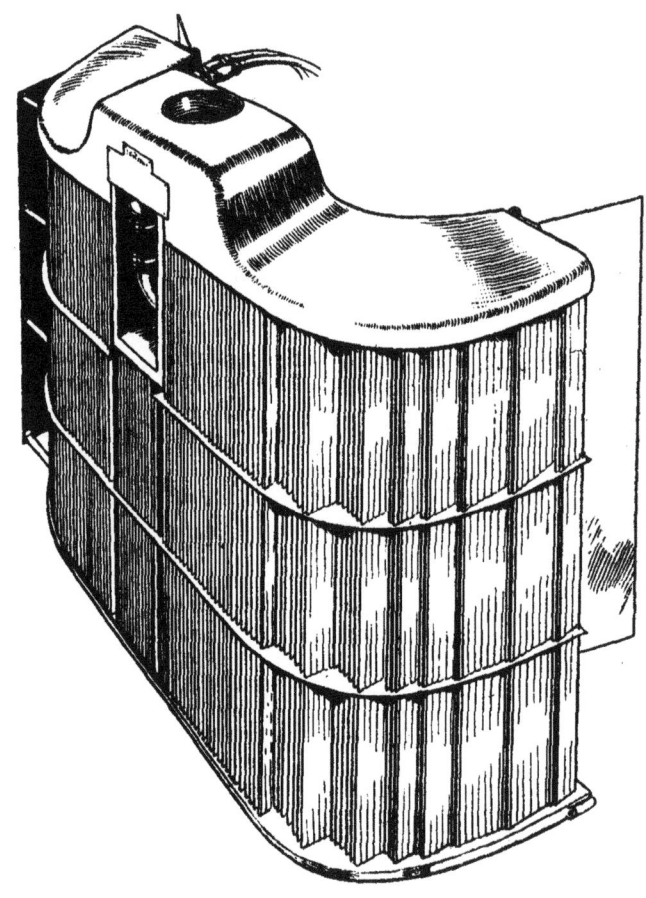

Fig. 11.

## PETROL SYSTEM.

As in the D VII. Fokker, both petrol tanks are inside the fuselage. It will be seen that the seat is placed rather far back, and in connection with this, it is remarked that the main petrol tank (sketched in Fig. 12) is placed low down in the fuselage underneath the rudder bar, and is covered with a 3-ply foot board. Its capacity is 16.1 galls. The auxiliary tank is slung from the gun bearers, as shown in Fig. 14, and has a capacity of 2.6 galls. This gives a total petrol capacity of approximately 18¾ galls. Both tanks work under pressure. The usual Mercedes oil tank is present, and holds, roughly, 2 galls.

The throttle is a simple lever, without quadrant or ratchet, which is coupled to the carburettor by light gauge steel tubing, and there is no sign of there having been any interconnected throttle on the control lever. The welded exhaust pipe points outwards and downwards, and is visible in several illustrations.

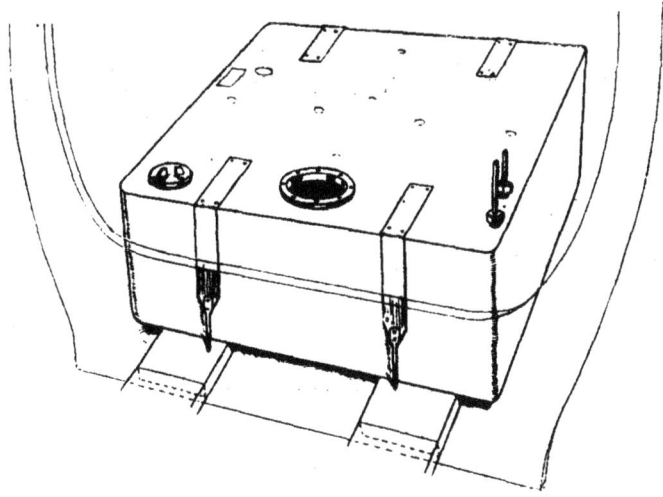

Fig. 12.

## CONTROLS.

The stick and its connections are both clearly explained by the sketch (Fig. 13). It will be noticed that only the gun triggers are found near the handles. The rudder bar is precisely similar to that of the D III Pfalz, and has the same adjustment. From the photographs it will be noticed that the cables are enclosed in the body for the greater part of their length and that the upper elevator cable passes right through the fixed tail plane. The aileron cables pass in the usual way through the lower wings, and are protected there by rolled tubes of varnished paper. The place where they leave the lower plane and pass upwards to the aileron lever is marked in the drawings and photographs and the pulleys at this point are of aluminium, and are neatly enclosed in cases of light-gauge sheet steel.

## ARMAMENT.

In common with the undercarriage and many instruments, both guns had been removed before the machine was inspected, but they were obviously of the Spandau type, fixed, and firing through the propeller path by the usual clutch and synchronising gear. The triggers are on the control lever, and are illustrated in Fig. 13. As in the Fokker biplane, two strong steel channels are fitted under the guns, and over the engine. They are visible in all three photographs, and in the scale drawings. The double ammunition box is of sheet aluminium, but has a tinplate top, and holds 400 rounds for each gun. It would appear that links were used between the cartridges, as no special receptacle for the usual web belt could be found. A link and cartridge-case deflector is fitted to the top of the cowling.

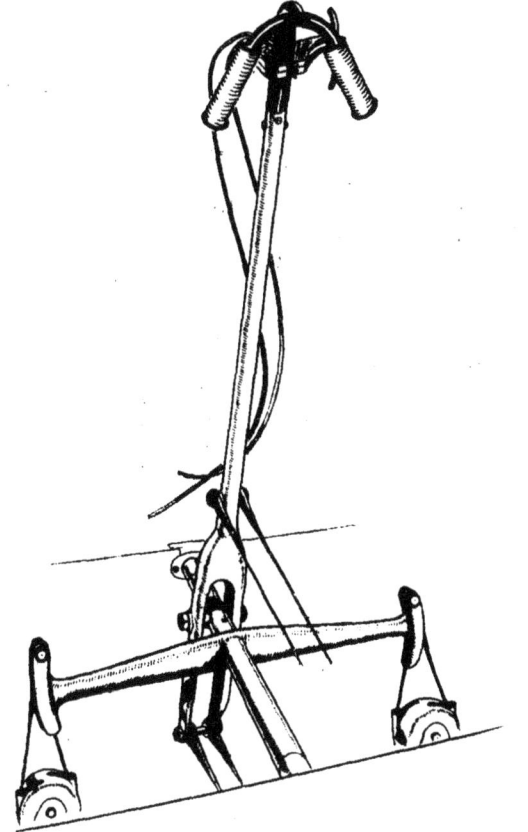

Fig. 13.

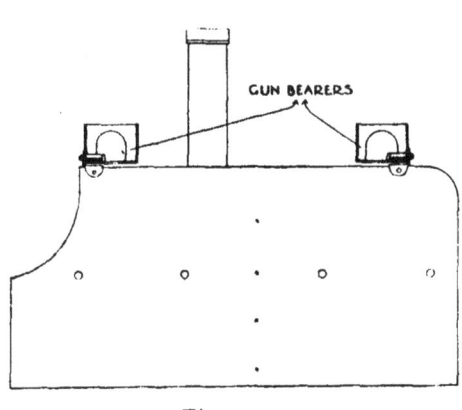

Fig. 14.

## INSTRUMENTS.

These were not salved, and all that can be definitely stated is that the compass was of the Pathfinder type, and was fixed inside the cockpit. No dashboard was used, but the instruments had been distributed around the cockpit. It is reported that the pilot was provided with a parachute, which was folded into the seat, and acted as a cushion, but these fittings were not salved.

## PROPELLER.

This is of Heine make, No. 26206; diameter 2,780, pitch 2,000. It has eight laminations of mahogany and walnut.

## FABRIC AND PAINTING.

The fabric is the usual colour-printed variety, and the body was painted dark purple from nose to rear of engine; bluish-grey to pilot's cockpit; and a dark green shading into a light pea-green extending to the tail. The fin and rudder are creamy-white, as is the part of the body above the tail planes, but the tail planes themselves, and the underneath portion of the body at the tail, are painted in broad stripes of alternate black and white. The photographs help to identify these various divisions.

## SCHEDULE OF PRINCIPAL WEIGHTS. (D XII Type.)

| | lbs. | oz. |
|---|---|---|
| Fuselage, without engine, guns, auxiliary tank or oil tank, but with main tank and tail skid | 257 | 0 |
| Starboard lower wing, with control cables, but no bracing wires. Only one side fabric covered | 46 | 0 |
| Upper wing, with bracing wires, but only one side fabric covered | 127 | 0 |
| One centre section M strut | 7 | 4 |
| Radiator | 44 | 8 |
| Brass oil tank | 5 | 1 |
| Auxiliary petrol tank | 7 | 8 |
| One outer N strut | 8 | 9 |
| One inner N strut | 10 | 6 |
| Fin (covered) | 3 | 2 |
| Aileron (covered) | 7 | 12 |
| Aileron hinge rod | 0 | 8 |
| 3-ply tail plane (partly estimated) | 19 | 0 |
| Aluminium nose cowl | 3 | 14 |
| Cockpit cowl and padding | 2 | 6 |
| One aluminium side cowl | 2 | 12 |
| Ammunition magazine | 7 | 12 |
| Two clutches for synchronising gear | 5 | 13 |
| Two gun channels | 5 | 5 |

The weights of the various components of the earlier Pfalz—the D III type—make an interesting comparison, and are given below:—

| | lbs. | ozs. |
|---|---|---|
| Fuselage, without engine, guns, or empennage, but with tanks and all fittings | 295 | 0 |
| One lower plane, covered, but without bracing wires | 49 | 0 |
| Complete upper plane, covered, with ailerons, bracing wires, radiator, and gravity tank | 225 | 0 |
| One centre section strut | 9 | 6 |
| Radiator | 37 | 3 |
| Brass oil tank | 3 | 2 |
| One U interplane strut | 8 | 13 |
| Aileron, covered | 10 | 14 |
| Fixed tailplanes, without fabric | 14 | 9 |
| Aluminium spinner | 1 | 7 |
| Cowl behind spinner | 2 | 13 |
| Exhaust pipes | 11 | 8 |
| Tail skid, bare | 5 | 0 |
| Elevator, without fabric | 9 | 0 |
| Rudder, with fabric | 6 | 13 |

G.T.C.,

Ap.D. (L.),

J. G. WEIR,

Brigadier-General,

Controller, Technical Department.

View from the front. Note radiator and sloping V struts.

Photograph of the machine as salved.

NOTE.—In all these illustrations the machine is shown resting on trolleys. The landing gear was not salved.

The port side of the D XII Pfalz.

From this photograph a good idea of the oval-sectioned body can be obtained.

The starboard side.　　Note Fokker-type struts.

Three-quarter rear view.

View from the rear.

Semi-plan view from behind.    Note shape of tail plane.

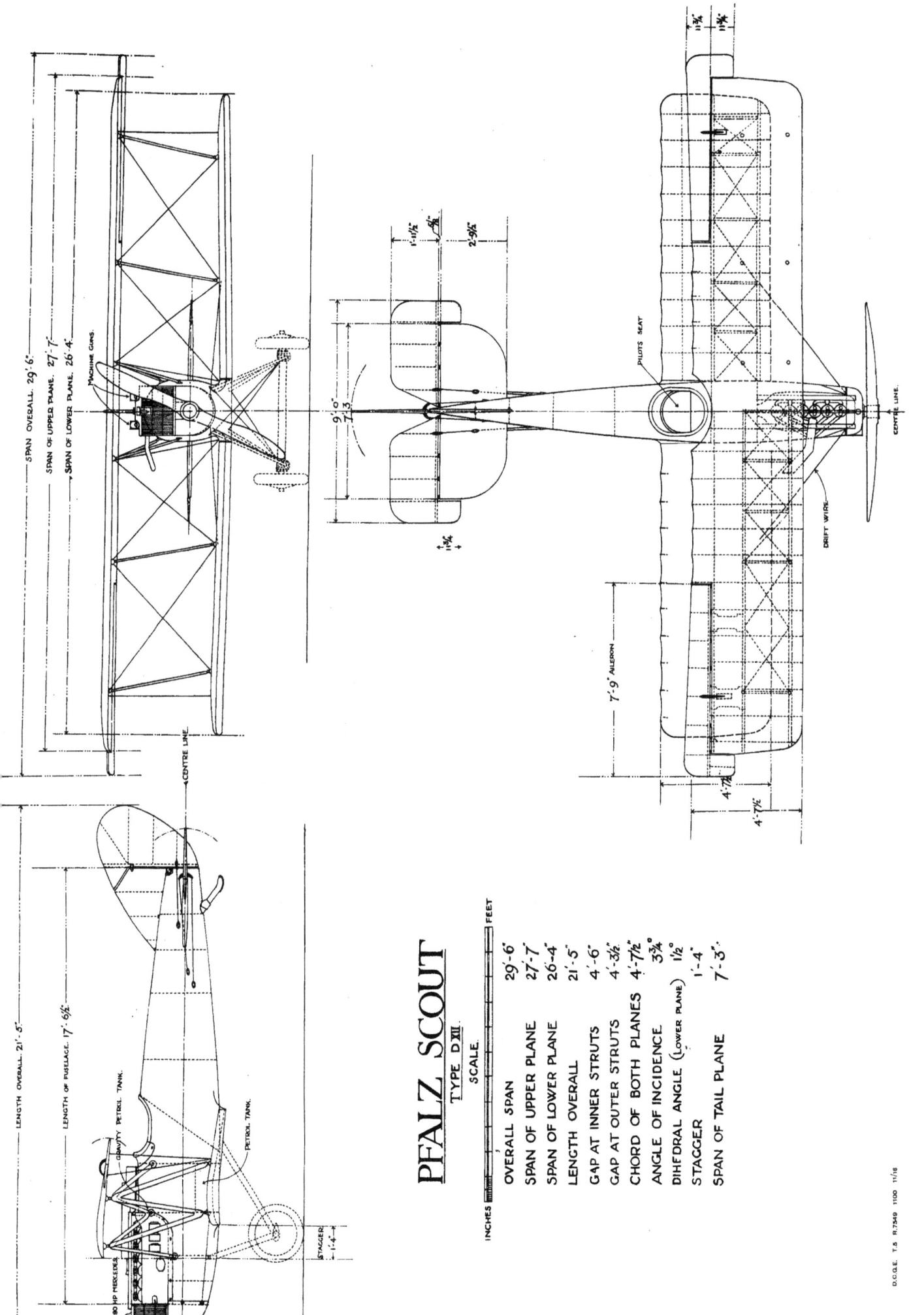

www.ingramcontent.com/pod-product-compliance
Ingram Content Group UK Ltd.
Pitfield, Milton Keynes, MK11 3LW, UK
UKHW051526180426
11947UKWH00019B/1595